D1456599

SPORTS FOR SPROUTS

Bicycle Riding

Tracy Nelson Maurer

ROURKE
PUBLISHING

www.rourkepublishing.com

111510

© 2011 Rourke Publishing LLC

All rights reserved. No part of this book may be reproduced or utilized in any form or by any means, electronic or mechanical including photocopying, recording, or by any information storage and retrieval system without permission in writing from the publisher.

www.rourkepublishing.com

The author gratefully acknowledges Shaun Murphy for his biking expertise and Megan Atwood for her kind project assistance.

Photo credits: All photo's © blue door publishing, except:
Cover © greenland; Title Page © Wendy Nero, Crystal Kirk, Leah-Anne Thompson, vnosokin, Gerville Hall, Rob Marmion; Page 3/4 © greenland; Page 7 © Fotokate; Page 11 © Rob Marmion; Page 20 © Dawnbal1; Page 22 © greenland, blue door publishing; Page 23 © Rob Marmion, blue door publishing

Editor: Jeanne Sturm

Cover and page design by Nicola Stratford, Blue Door Publishing

Library of Congress Cataloging-in-Publication Data

Maurer, Tracy, 1965-
 Bicycle riding / Tracy Nelson Maurer.
    p. cm. -- (Sports for sprouts)
 Includes bibliographical references and index.
 ISBN 978-1-61590-234-7 (Hard cover) (alk. paper)
 ISBN 978-1-61590-474-7 (Soft cover)
 1. Cycling--Juvenile literature. I. Title.
 GV1043.5.M356 2011
 796.6--dc22
                                        2010009020

Rourke Publishing
Printed in the United States of America, North Mankato, Minnesota
033010
033010LP

www.rourkepublishing.com - rourke@rourkepublishing.com
Post Office Box 643328 Vero Beach, Florida 32964

I ride my
bicycle safely.

I wear a **helmet** and bright clothes.

I make sure my feet can reach the ground.

My **training wheels** help me balance.

Learning to ride takes **practice**.

We ride on the **bike path.**

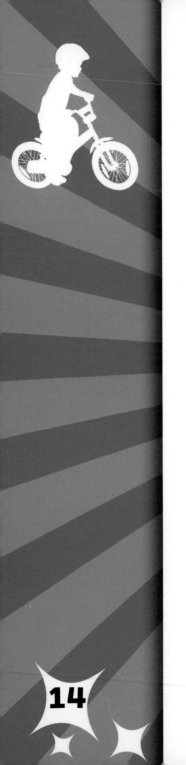

We play follow
the **leader**.

We stop and look both ways.

We **signal** our turn.

Riding bicycles safely keeps the fun rolling!

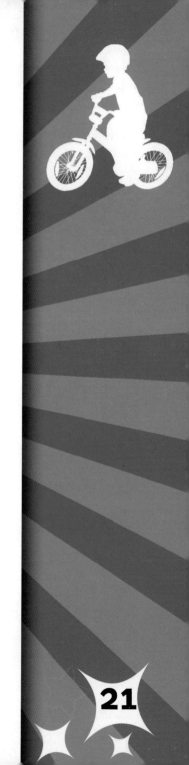

Picture Glossary

bike path (BIKE PATH): A bike path allows riders to travel without much or any motorized vehicle traffic.

helmet (HEL-met): A helmet protects a rider's brain from injury.

leader (LEE-dur): A leader in a bike game chooses where to ride and how fast. The other riders do what the leader does.

practice (PRAK-tiss): To practice, or do something many times, helps improve a person's skills.

signal (SIG-nul): A signal shows other riders and vehicle drivers if the bicyclist plans to turn left or right.

training wheels (TRANE-ing WEELZ): Training wheels are a set of small wheels that help bike riders stay balanced.

Index

balance 9

bike path   13

feet 6

helmet   5

leader   14

practice   10

signal   18

Websites

www.ibike.org/education/teaching-kids.htm

www.familyfun.go.com/playtime/take-a-bike-hike-701910/

kidshealth.org/kid/watch/out/bike_safety.html

About the Author

Tracy Nelson Maurer loves to play with her two children and husband in their neighborhood near Minneapolis, Minnesota. She holds an MFA in Writing for Children & Young Adults from Hamline University, and has written more than 70 books for young readers.